THINGS
I WISH
JESUS SAID

Barbara F. Nixon

For Amanda Grace and Stephanie Kate

ACKNOWLEDGMENTS

I have always been reluctant to publish my writing. It makes it so very permanent. But, during the past three years, as I have read and reread, edited and rewritten the ideas in this book, I find I stand by the theological perspectives expressed here. This is largely due to two congregations who first listened to these thoughts as sermons. I thank the precious people of Junction City United Methodist Church in Oregon and Hillview United Methodist Church in Boise, Idaho, for engaging these ideas as I began to give them voice and for exploring them with curiosity and candor. You have given me courage and clarity.

I offered a rough draft of this book to small groups in a variety of church settings to see what might happen, asking only that they offer some feedback about their experiences and their discussions. Several groups accepted the offer and contributed input to various ways. I thank you all. I took your comments seriously as I continued my work, and I made many changes based on your suggestions. I am especially grateful to discussion groups in First United Methodist Church (UMC) of Corvallis, OR, King of Glory Lutheran Church (Boise, ID), Morningside UMC (Salem, OR), Sweethome UMC (OR), Mira Vista United Church of Christ (Richmond, CA), Tigard

UMC (OR) and Aptos Community UMC (CA). Your detailed input proved especially useful.

Several individuals have offered encouragement, wisdom and practical support as I worked on *Things I Wish Jesus Said.* To Richard Linford, Teresa Salyer, Barbara Schultz, Brooke Collison, Elizabeth Claman, Robert Shively, Geoff Stewart, Todd Lesh, Jo-Ann Kachigian and Jon Brown, I give my heartfelt thanks for the particular ways you each helped this project along.

I thank Dr. Brett Strobel for providing the backbone for *Ideas for Additional Reading,* listed at the end of the book. Your help with this made a big difference.

Finally, I thank you, the reader, for reading *Things I Wish Jesus Said.* In offering my perspectives, my hope is that you will have an opportunity to examine, explore, clarify, confirm, express or otherwise claim for yourself beliefs and ideas that honestly inform your own faith.

TABLE OF CONTENTS

INTRODUCTION

It seems like so very many years ago now, a retired semi-nary professor handed me a book by an author he thought I would appreciate. We were members of the same church, where I served as program director. We had shared several conversations about the nature of God, the life of Jesus, the Trinity—you name it. He knew that I was both curious and confused. I, in my thirties, was having a sort of spiritual "midlife" crisis. There were so many troubling beliefs and notions I had been taught—beliefs I had held on to out of love for God, out of love for people who, through the years, had been Church to me, out of fear for my soul.

It was all or nothing—at least that is how it seemed.

It didn't matter that I could not make sense out of HOW Jesus had saved me by dying on a cross two thousand years ago.

It did not matter that I was fuzzy about what I had done that created the need for this particular salvation.

It did not matter if some stories and sayings in the Bible did not seem to ring true.

It did not matter what crazy thoughts and questions popped into my head and heart.

I did not think it was possible to hang on to Jesus and stay in the good graces of a God I knew was real if I doubted or discarded these teachings. I just needed to believe...

So, the retired professor handed me a book and I read it—and it changed my life. It freed me to trust the deep "truths" of scriptures while still being able to have a skeptical attitude here or there—anywhere within it. I saw there was a place for critical thinking!

I began to trust, for the first time in a mature way, that the love of God did not hinge on my knowing or somehow figuring out exact, correct beliefs. As I allowed myself to consider God, Jesus, and the teachings of the Church without blind obedience, I found my faith did not diminish.

My faith blossomed.

Every time I allowed myself to ask a question, a new horizon opened before me.

This is the journey that continues for me to this day...

Let a question arise; see where it takes you; go there...don't be afraid.

And it all started with that book:

The Christian Agnostic by Dr. Leslie Weatherhead.

Weatherhead was a well-known and highly respected British Methodist preacher and author. Written in 1965 after his retirement, his book seemed almost heretical in its time, making the claim that sometimes the long-held beliefs attached to Christianity could actually interfere with God's message of love brought to us in Jesus Christ. It was okay to question, to doubt, to challenge what many Christians assume to be true. This was a courageous undertaking on his part, one for which I am personally quite grateful.

Not so many years after reading *The Christian Agnostic*, I headed off to seminary with the blessings and encouragement of my home church—ready to expand that questioning, doubting process.

Those years took me further into what I can only describe as my "call" to ministry. My faith, my understanding and my excitement grew. I now serve as an ordained elder in the United Methodist Church. And, as I have served churches as pastor, I have done my best to encourage the same questioning process that continues to deepen and define my own faith.

Contrary to what many might say, I think it is not at all easy to read the Bible and come away with clear understandings of who Jesus is, what he teaches and how we can apply it to our lives. It takes hard work.

Time and again I see people freed by this work of letting their questions rise, seeing where they lead and exploring those spaces fearlessly— together. This work is, I think, what it takes to be a faithful follower of Jesus in the twenty-first century, two thousand years after he walked the earth.

A while back, I sat in my office, pondering again how frustrating it is to thoughtfully challenge us all to do this work, and I spoke out loud, "You know, Jesus, there are a few things I sure wish you had said—things that would make it a lot simpler to follow you in OUR time—things that would lay to rest some of the ways you may be misunderstood."

And thus was born the sermon series called "Things I Wish Jesus Said." I have adapted it here in hopes of opening some thought-provoking conversation. Perhaps it offers a little fresh air and maybe a little freedom—the way *The Christian Agnostic* did for me all those years ago.

Thank you, Dr. Paul Radamacher, for handing me that book. Thank you, Dr. Leslie Weatherhead, for writing it.

CHAPTER 1 THINGS I WISH JESUS SAID:

"DON'T BELIEVE EVERYTHING YOU READ."

We Christians sometimes hold some pretty crazy, mixed-up ideas about God. In my life as a pastor, I have seen the same theological confusions rise again and again. People repeat things they have learned in childhood, as if they were indisputable facts. They get stuck, rather than freed, by the beliefs that govern their lives. They feel betrayed and confused when God does not "behave" as they expect. They become fearful when God is interpreted for them as angry and judgmental, afraid they may be condemned forever if they don't believe the right things.

We know the basics:

Jesus died for MY sins...

> He suffered on the cross for ME. All that matters is to accept the gift of his death on my behalf. Then resurrection is mine.

God has a plan for my life...

> I need to discover God's will for me personally and seek to let that will govern my every decision.

Jesus is God...

> and so is the Father/creator of all—and the Holy Spirit. Jesus is also God's Son—it's complicated!

The love of God is yours if you believe the right things...

> and you are forever condemned if you don't.

Expect a miracle...

> Enough prayer, the right prayer, a good life—God can reward these things with miracles. These are signs of God's particular blessing.

The list is much longer and there are many variations. The list often goes unexamined and unquestioned for so many of us.

We have been told that these beliefs are necessary if we want to be saved. This is what it means to be a Christian. Questioning these long-held basics is unnecessary—actually, unwelcome.

To doubt these beliefs is to doubt God.

That makes for a pretty big barrier to deep inquiry into the foundations of one's faith! Still, I have found that when an invitation is extended, there is great hunger to pursue such exploration. Many of us who follow Jesus do not actually hold to these "right" beliefs at all, but we aren't sure how to proceed from that awareness or where that takes us. What can we claim and how do we get there?

First and foremost, this exploration requires a careful study of the Bible. This, in itself, can be quite challenging. One can lift quotes from here and there and make a case for all sorts of particulars, ranging from how God will end the world to how God anoints those who handle snakes and drink poison. One can find several different ways to understand the nature of Jesus and his relationship to God. One can find all sorts of laws and rules, some of them self-contradictory. "Careful study" means one has to get to know the Bible well enough to see it not just as pieces but as a whole.

The Bible is centrally important in clarifying one's faith. At the same time, the Bible is hugely problematic!

Sometimes I wish Jesus had said, "Don't believe everything you read."

As a pastor, I make it a point not to quote the Bible. I read verses and passages from the Bible when I preach on Sunday mornings. I lead Bible studies in which we read verses and explore them at length. We talk about the stories and ideas that fill its pages, especially those that speak of Jesus's life. I just don't *quote* the Bible to make a point when talking with people. I think this is wise for many reasons:

The problem of authorship

There are those who understand the Bible to be the direct word of God—flawless in every way that could matter.

There are others who would say that God is not exactly the author, but that the Bible is God's inspired word to us—those who did write it had a kind of direct line to God as source.

From either of these understandings comes the view that the Bible is authoritative, accurate and contains all God would have us know in order to live fully.
In a very real sense, the Bible is God's word.

These perspectives make KNOWING the Bible incredibly important—in order to be clear about what must be believed and how one must live to be saved.

There are still others (and I include myself among them) who believe the Bible documents how God has been experienced by people—many different people—over an extended period of time.

This means that what we have in the Bible are *various* views of God and how God has moved and interacted with humanity. From this perspective, there is much insight and knowledge to be gleaned from the dozens of distinct and complementary books that comprise the Bible.

It is all held as sacred, but not all accounts are considered historically accurate (meaning that myth and metaphor hold an important place).

> In a very real sense,
> *God has been interpreted for us by those who authored the Bible.*

This view, too, suggests that Bible study is very important, but not for proof of anything. Rather, the Bible is studied in order to discover how God was experienced in another time, place and context and how these experiences inform our lives.

There are, no doubt, many variations on these views of authorship. All of this makes "Bible-quoting" tricky. It raises the question: who exactly is being quoted?

> God's self?
> A scribe for God?
> A faith-filled, ancient peasant?
> Jesus himself?

While quoting can be very affirming among people who share the same view of biblical authorship, it all shifts when we try to talk across our differences. The person who uses a biblical quote to make some sort of point may have an entirely different perspective on authorship than the person listening.

The "proof-text" problem

Another reason not to quote the Bible is the way it is so often used to prove a point. I refuse to get into "proof-text" arguments. You may know the kind I'm talking about—a person attempts to make an entire case against someone or a case for something by quoting a verse or brief passage from the Bible.

I have found there can never be any real exchange of ideas between people, even with the best of intentions, when anyone simply quotes the Bible to make a point.

People who believe the Bible literally are most inclined to use it as proof—

after all, it is God's word.

This, in itself, closes the door on any broader conversation about how the Bible might inform us in different ways—if viewed as less authoritative.

And even biblical authority can be proved by quoting the Bible itself! (2 Timothy 3:16-17 is a favorite.) In my experience, attempts at conversation that involve proof-texting aren't conversations at all.

> They are more like contests with winners and losers.
> Worse still, they become battles, with the Bible as the weapon of choice.

Clearly, I am not a biblical literalist. Many who believe that every word in the Bible is true readily quote it as the final word on just about any subject. I have stopped arguing in these situations. Arguing simply makes me party to a war of words.

Deserving something more

I hold that we all deserve something more than simple Bible-quoting to address things that truly matter. I see all of us who find the Bible sacred as having a serious, collective responsibility to bring our knowledge, our reason and our experience to an understanding of scripture for our time. It can be abusive, disrespectful and irresponsible to ignore all the resources God gives us to better understand this ancient book.

"Don't believe everything you read."

Obviously, Jesus had no need to say this in his time. The written word was valued in his day, but the Bible as we know it certainly did not exist, and the problems that plague Christians with understanding it have arisen over time.

The Bible is not God. In my experience as a pastor, I have learned there is a great hunger for a more skeptical, more informed, more nuanced study of scripture. People come to new, deep faith understandings when they have permission and encouragement to ask questions and challenge their own beliefs rather than simply fall back on familiar quotes and explanations.

They now appreciate that ancient people told precious stories to explain creation and disasters. It is not necessary for these stories to be historically or scientifically factual for these accounts to be truly sacred and full of meaning.

They see it is important to remember that Jesus, no matter how holy, how one with God, was also a man of his time who knew nothing about chaos theory and probably thought, as did people of his day, that heaven was about three miles above the earth.

They accept with appreciation that the gospel accounts of Jesus's birth, death and resurrection and many of his words and stories differ tremendously in detail. They find themselves less concerned about "facts" and more concerned about the meaning and experiences offered in these accounts.

We deserve the riches that can come from letting the Bible speak in all the ways it can—without reducing it to quotable "sound bites" that dismantle or ignore the bigger, more powerful sweep of these beautiful texts.

Misquoting scripture

A purely practical reason why I don't quote the Bible is that I cannot be trusted to do so. If my capacity to remember the words of scripture accurately is any indication of what's out there, then Bible-quoting simply cannot be trusted!

I have personally heard the Bible credited with Shakespeare and other literary figures, and with the great pearls of wisdom "a bird in the hand is worth two in the bush," and "a stitch in time saves nine."

Then there are the vague, "almost"-quoters who offer biblical truths in the forms of questions—

> "Doesn't the Bible say, 'God will never give you more than you can bear'?"

> "Didn't Jesus say, 'Homosexuals are going to hell'?"

Sometimes these misquotes are innocent enough.

> Sometimes they are a lazy attempt to use the Bible to bolster a prejudice.

> Let's face it—just mentioning the Bible is enough
> to give an idea or question the guise of authority.

Quoting Jesus

Quoting Jesus is particularly problematic for all the reasons I've explored above. Add to this that his words carry great authority with Christians, even though more and more scholars agree that not every word attributed to Jesus was spoken by him. The gospels, written across many years after Jesus left the earth, have him saying very different things or similar things with slightly different implications or the same things in different settings. The longer Christians waited for Jesus's return, the more elaborate and "Christianized" the stories and words attributed to him became.

With this in mind, I recognize the irony of wishing Jesus had said, "Don't believe everything you read." But the longer I serve as a pastor, the more I appreciate how challenging it is to navigate the Bible, how difficult it is to offer people a counterpoint to the Bible-quoting theology so many have been offered throughout their lives, how important it is to read the Bible with care.

I am a fan of what John Wesley taught—that scripture needs to be interpreted and explored through the lenses of tradition/history (where past understandings have taken us), as well as through our reason and experience. You certainly don't have to be a Methodist to value these tools and appreciate how necessary it is to approach the Bible more holistically and critically. Other denominations have similar tools and strategies for reading the Bible. It takes effort—focused effort.

Things I Wish Jesus Said is consequently not so much a book about studying the Bible proper. It is more of an encouragement to lift the value of exploring tradition/history, reason and experience in our lives as followers of Jesus—to find our way to beliefs we can truly call our own and, of course, to not believe everything you read.

Carol cont' writ

Questions to consider:

1) Describe an experience you have had with someone who quoted the Bible in conversation. How did you respond?
2) Why is Bible knowledge and study important to you?
3) If you agree that "proof-texting" is unacceptable, what do you think are appropriate/meaningful ways to reference the Bible when speaking with people about things that matter to you?
4) Are there occasions/circumstances when it is appropriate to quote meaningful passages and verses?
5) Name a few places in our culture where the Bible is referenced to push an agenda. How might the conversation be different without the Bible being used in this way?

In your own words: How do you describe the Bible and its purpose?

because I am learning enough to know why I didn't ever ~~believe~~ believe everything I read & ~~to have faith in~~ ~~understand~~ to make my own judgements, I'm beginning to understand why I ma~~ke~~ that particular call (Truth ~~fiction~~ metaphor) (~~important~~ to me or not) (~~important vs unimportant~~ acceptable to me or not). and I have faith in my own judgement ~~in this~~ as it applies to me.

Chapter 2 Things I Wish Jesus Said:

"It's not about me."

It is generally accepted that Jesus's ministry lasted about three years. While the details vary from gospel to gospel, we can, from these writings, get a pretty clear sense of how Jesus spent his time.

He healed people—
all kinds of people with all kinds of struggles. No matter which gospel you read, you will find stories of his amazing power and willingness to heal brokenness.

He trained and nurtured leaders—
leaders who he chose from amongst the people. He loved them and trusted them with his message, even with their obvious flaws and weaknesses.

He engaged skeptics and adversaries—
While the poor and oppressed seemed to flock to his presence, others who felt threatened by his authority tried to trick and challenge his power and wisdom. He always responded. Sometimes he intentionally defied the letter of the law, pointing instead to the spirit of it.

We know he spent time alone—
Sometimes the gospel writers give readers glimpses of these times, showing us an earnest Jesus communing with his Father, God.

Jesus spent a lot of his time teaching people—
wherever and whenever crowds gathered. He spoke of the kingdom of God. He often talked about the kingdom in parables, trying to bring into focus a reality that already existed in and through him—a kingdom that was truly hard to imagine and was threatening to those who held earthly power over the lives of others. When Jesus taught people, he sometimes spoke of his incredible, deep connection to God and how much power there was when you lived in that love. I like to say that Jesus was so open to God, so full of God's love, that when we see Jesus, we see God. Another way to describe this might be that if prayer is a state in which one's heart is open to God, then Jesus lived in a constant state of prayer.

This is how I would describe what Jesus did. This is how he spent his time—what he offered with his life—what he wanted us to know.

This is why Jesus is incredibly important. In him, we see what the love of God looks like in human form. We see what is possible and how different the world is when we share in that love. Jesus wasn't just merely a model or example—

> He was a profound agent of change, in and for the world.

> He opened a door and love flowed—
> through him, to anyone—everyone.

He encouraged people to trust that they, too, were capable of doing amazing things through God's love.

It is important to recall the cultural, historical context for Jesus's ministry. The Jews were an oppressed people, living under Roman rule. Uprisings and hope of uprisings against Rome were an established part of peasant life. Some who followed Jesus thought he would be the sort of revolutionary who would bring the fall of Rome. Some were disappointed he was not that kind of rebel. But Roman authorities executed Jesus because they thought he was that dangerous. Even after Jesus's death and resurrection, there was (and, I have to say, still is) an image of Jesus as the great conqueror who would bring justice and end oppression by massive and permanent destruction of the wicked.

After he walked the earth, those who followed Jesus continued to worship in the Temple side by side with those who did not see Jesus as the Messiah—as the anointed one who had come to save the people. These Christians, as they came to be called, were a relatively small band that included a few followers who were not Jews by heritage. These "gentiles" had begun to embrace the roots of this man Jesus, whom they had decided to follow. For a time, Jews, Jewish Christians and gentile Christians alike all worshipped the one, very same God together—waiting, hoping, praying for justice.

But about forty years after Jesus lived, Rome had had enough upheaval and rebellion. Soldiers marched through Jerusalem, destroying the city and leveling the Temple. This devastation sent everyone into the countryside, to the smaller towns and villages. And in these settings, with everyone living in great distress and fear, an inevitable split unfolded. In 88 CE, Christians were officially expelled from the synagogues. All connections were severed. It was made clear that Christians were no longer considered children of God and should make no claim on the God of Abraham, Isaac and Moses. This was a bitter split and the gospel that emerges from the heat of this split is the Gospel of John.

When we know this background, we can see more clearly why it reads so differently than the other three (synoptic) gospels. Christians will indeed make their claim on the God of Israel! The gospel opens with those poetic, powerful words:

> In the beginning was the Word, and the Word was with God, and the Word was God. All things came into being through him, and without him, not one thing came into being. (John 1:1, 3a NRSV)

These verses make a claim for Jesus as the Word—that he was there prior to and was indeed the driving force of God's creation—BEFORE and more important than Abraham, Isaac and Jacob.

16

Our Jesus trumps the patriarchs!!

The Jesus of John's gospel is barely human. From the opening verses to the close of the gospel, Jesus is utterly in charge—knowing and managing all that unfolds. He has, quite literally, dropped down to earth from on high. Read the powerful "I am" statements attributed to him throughout the gospel:

> I am the bread of life... I am the light of the world... I am the door for the sheep... I am the good shepherd... I am the resurrection and the life... I am the way, the truth and the life... I am the vine, you are the branches.

The writer of John's gospel has taken the Hebrew name for God—"I am" or "I am that I am"—and has elevated Jesus in an unprecedented way. For Christians, Jesus can speak as and for the one true God!

Most Bible scholars today agree that the writer of John's gospel is not quoting Jesus with these extraordinary words. Neither is the writer a liar. It was an acceptable practice in those times to create stories and words in this very fashion. And this early Christian community, wounded by being expelled and set apart, was doing its best to demonstrate what they knew of this remarkable Jesus. If you compare the earliest gospel, Mark, to the last gospel, John, you will see the shift from a more human Jesus, who became open to God, to a more godly Jesus, who chose to be human.

This struggle to comprehend and describe the unique beauty of Jesus's life and message has been ongoing within the Bible itself and throughout the history of Christianity. The fledgling Church needed to understand God the creator, the role of Jesus and the nature of the Holy Spirit in some unified way. The concept of the Trinity rose from an attempt to hold in tension the different ways God is present.

Somehow in that struggle, over time, Jesus, and his message of God's love, has moved to the top of this trinitarian construct. As twenty-first-century Christians, we like to say that Jesus is on par with/one with the "Father" and the "Holy Spirit." But many Christian books and music, as well as Christian broadcasting these days, suggest something else.

Look at so many of our church songs and hymns. Jesus is celebrated, elevated and named as the lone ingredient in a path to God. Jesus is thanked and glorified for blessings of all sorts.

We pray to him. We pray in his name.
We praise him. We thank God for him and give him credit for all the good stuff.
Somehow we have turned God—the source of all that is holy—into Jesus's dad!

That's why I wish Jesus had said,

"It's not about me."
If he were standing here today, I think he would say that it is always and only about the love of God.

He would tell us that all he ever did was point to the Father—
that even when he connected himself to the Father, it was to
show us what was possible.

He would remind us that he taught about the love of God and
God's kingdom that exists in and among us, no matter what
our earthly circumstances.

He would remind us of his humanity, of the power of God's
love that is present in our lives, waiting for release.

> "It's not about me. This is what happens when God is
> expressed through any of us!"

Jesus did not ask people to worship him. He didn't ask to be
lifted up and set apart. He didn't seek godliness for himself.

*If we end our journey of faith worshipping at the feet of Jesus, we stop
short of the fullness of what it means to follow him—
because Jesus was pointing to God.*

When we stop short, it is like looking at a mirror and admir-
ing the glass and the frame instead of looking into it to see
what is revealed about you.

It's like opening a hymnal and appreciating the paper and
how beautiful the notes look on the page, without hearing
the music. Or letting someone else sing, instead of singing for
yourself.
Somehow we have allowed ourselves to think that the life of
Jesus is so elevated, so separate and so different from our own

that IIE satisfies all that God might want from humanity. There is nothing for us to do but worship him.

I wish Jesus had said, "It's not about me. It's about you— how much God loves you—how full God wants YOUR life to be—what your life can mean for the world!"

But it has been almost two thousand years since Jesus walked the earth. He could not know how time would shape and interpret his ministry. It is important for us to read scripture and look at Jesus's life with fresh eyes, open hearts and open minds.

The first step is to risk letting go of what we think we know, what we have assumed and how we have been taught. If we have faith in this love that Jesus taught and lived—if we can look where Jesus always pointed—our journey with him can take us further than our imaginings.

Questions to consider:

1) How do you describe the relationship between God and Jesus?
2) In what ways does the portrayal in this chapter challenge your personal experience/understanding of Jesus?
3) Can YOU be like Jesus? Why or why not?
4) What might be at risk/at stake in accepting the idea that it's not about Jesus but rather about you?

In your own words: Who is Jesus in relationship to God?

CHAPTER 3 THINGS I WISH JESUS SAID:

"I DIDN'T COME TO SAVE YOU."

If you were to ask random people on the street, "What do Christians believe?" you would, no doubt, hear some variations on these responses:

> Christians believe that Jesus had to die on the cross in order to save them from their sins.

> Christians believe that Jesus is their savior. They have to believe in him in order to be right with God.

> Christians believe that anyone who doesn't believe Jesus can save them will go to hell. Those who do believe in Jesus will go to heaven. God will choose.

The belief that Jesus came into the world to SAVE us is pretty central to the lives of most Christians. For many, this belief is of ultimate importance because people's eternal lives hang in the balance. It is a huge relief to trust that Jesus can set things right between God and us. No wonder he is praised and worshipped.

Accepting Jesus as your savior means you will live happily *forever* after.

Still, I wish Jesus had said, "I didn't come to save you."

I say this because there are some dark beliefs wrapped up inside this happy salvation ending. We have to look at these carefully.

First of all, this thinking that Jesus must save us from our sins so we may live in heaven implies that everything in this life is just some sort of test or screening before you get to enter the REALLY GOOD life—forever.

That further implies that the goal of this life is to
    a) be saved yourself, and
    b) then save as many other people as possible.

It's pretty much all or nothing—someone is either saved or not.

Based on the numbers of people subscribing to the various major world religions, and the numbers of us who may not hold the exactly right beliefs about Jesus, most of us are not saved.

Alas, it seems most of us are going to hell.

And that brings me to a second dark belief wrapped up in this perspective. If salvation through Jesus is essential to save us from hell, then the God who has placed all of this in motion is a God who is content to let most of us burn forever.

Forgiveness for all our sins and harmful ways IS CONDITIONAL!

You must know of and adhere to "right beliefs" about Jesus. Otherwise, God's love and forgiveness are not available to you. It is troubling to see Jesus's life and teachings interpreted this way.

Gone is anything about justice for the poor, healing for the sick, care for the outcast.

Gone is the whole concept of the Kingdom of God, in which we participate through our loving actions on behalf of others.

Gone is the invitation to discover what it is like to live in this world trusting that God loves us without conditions.

All that matters is our answer to the question:

"Do you believe Jesus died to save you from your sins?"

God will determine the truth of your answer, the nature of your beliefs and seal your eternal fate in some final judgment.

This makes for an incredibly small and narrow view of God's intentions for our existence. And there is more to be said about this God of judgment—a third dark belief. This need to believe in the saving power of Jesus through his death on the cross holds, at its core, a belief that God requires a sacrifice.

God requires a sacrifice full of pain and suffering—in order to be a loving God.
Someone must pay or God cannot love us.

This is pretty nasty stuff.

One could argue this sounds like glorified child abuse—to make one especially beloved, innocent and enlightened child take the punishment for the other kids.

One could argue that the God who acts this way is not a loving God at all.

Summarizing Jesus's life and teachings with the phrase "*Jesus came to save us,*" as it has come to be understood by so many in our time, not only diminishes the vision of what is possible when a loving God reigns—it actually demonizes God.

It is this punishment-based view of the saving Jesus that makes me wish he had said, "I didn't come to save you." If we step away from this fear-inspired view of Jesus, we can be reminded that the whole notion of a messiah was based on the promise of one who would come to save the Jews from their oppressors (of which there had been many) and open up for them a better life—on earth. Those who understood Jesus in this way assumed he would take on their captors, the Roman Empire.

Jesus actually did this in a very real sense—his ideas about the Kingdom of God proved to be more of a threat than those of many revolutionaries in his time. But his nonviolent message of this kingdom in their midst was not easily understood or embraced, even by those who faithfully followed Jesus. After his death and resurrection, many of his followers thought Jesus would come back and put a violent end to their enemies. Ultimately, they would be saved from their captors and live under God's rule with Jesus on the throne. (I still hear loud echoes of this thinking in the twenty-first century.)

If we can let go of this violent view of a "saving" Jesus AND the notion that he will come again and mete out eternal penalties for those who fail, we can see his hopeful message of freedom and joy—of forgiveness and possibility, even in the midst of difficulties—then—now—always.

We can see that our very existence is how God expresses and experiences love.

I believe this big, unconditional love is Jesus's message to us.

Let me be clear—

This good news of God's love CAN and DOES indeed save us—from guilt, shame, loneliness, addictions, destructive behavior, despair, depression, sin in its many forms, fears of many kinds—even death itself.

But being saved is not the point.

The point is always what happens next.

If you stop at "being saved," it's like having money in the bank that you never spend.

It's like having your sight restored and then sitting in a dark room.

I think of the story in Matthew's gospel of Jesus walking on the water and Peter giving it a try. He struggles and begins to sink. Jesus saves him—rescues him from drowning. But that is not where the story ends. Peter does not spend the rest of his life sitting gratefully in the boat. He rises up to be an amazing and courageous leader. He becomes part of the good news, too.

Jesus came offering life in God's love—God's kingdom. We can be grateful that his life and teachings do save us from all kinds of destruction.

But the point of it all is what happens next.

And that means that you and I can actually be creating more good news and become part of the story ourselves…

I think ~~God that~~ Jesus came to give us
the knowledge of what is possible &
appropriate ~~between us~~ between us & God.

(19)

Questions to consider:

Trying to live as a "Christian" as possible. Not being saved for sure

1) What most defines "being a Christian" from your perspective?

2) Have your views of Jesus ever been challenged by fellow Christians who don't believe you "have it right"? How can/do you respond?

3) If your salvation is not the point, what is the role of salvation in your life? What might "what happens next" look like?

4) Do you trust that God's love and forgiveness are absolutely unconditional? What are the implications of "yes" or "no" as an answer?

In your own words: What does the phrase "being saved" mean to you?

I have never felt like I needed to be saved — Saved from what?

Any God I wanted to be with? (what) wouldn't think like that.

what did he do? make a mistake when he created people + the several thousand years into it he relents or realizes its unfixable + sends his son here to give us a way to fix his own mistake?

I don't think there is any salvation. maybe just learning to live better + better act more like Christ.

Chapter 4 Things I Wish Jesus Said:

"God does not have a plan for your life."

The church's newspaper advertisement reads
something like this:
God has a plan for each and every one of us.
Join us Sunday—
Hear Pastor Steve
explain how
YOU can fix your spot on the map of God's will!!

If we attend Pastor Steve's church this Sunday, my guess is we would learn, first of all, that the most essential part of God's plan for our lives is to secure our places in heaven by turning our lives over to Jesus. But if we attended Pastor Steve's church week after week, I think we would gradually see all that is implied in that simple phrase: God has a plan for your life.

Most likely, we would be advised to pray ALWAYS for God to reveal His (sic) will in all major decisions. We would be encouraged to examine all that happens in our lives in terms of how God's will is being taught or revealed, especially when things get tough. God is in control. God has a plan. This can be understood in two very different ways: either prayerfully discern God's plan in some specific ways and act accordingly, or simply live moment to moment trusting that whatever is going on somehow IS God's plan, in which case you will be able to see it in hindsight. That pretty much covers everything and it all happens for a reason, known or unknown.

From this "God-the-micromanager" model, I hear Christians ask God to choose not only the fate of their unborn child, but the kind of car they should buy as well. I hear faithful followers say that they will someday understand why God needed their child in heaven more than they needed him on earth. The same people who prayed for God to send them their spouse can be found praying about what to buy a friend for a birthday present. I hear Christians trying to discover the lessons they are being taught through God bringing an illness or other crises into their lives. Followers will not only pray about whether or not to build a new church, they will pray about the color of the carpet as well. No decision, no circumstance, no shift in the road is too great or small to be understood as an occasion for personal discernment as to God's plan in the matter.

Somehow we have thoroughly personalized the concept of God's will into this not-so-carefully examined view, that, in order to be in a right relationship with God, God must be in the driver's seat—not only driving, but building the roads and directing traffic as well. This is a far cry from an understanding that God holds the Big Picture—what I call a VISION for our lives—while we are free to shape our lives and, of course, the lives of those around us. I see this vision as what Jesus shared about the Kingdom of God: Jesus invites and seeks our participation in God's overarching will. I understand the will of God to be this vision: that creation can express all the love and beauty that is God's very nature. I think this vision gets lost when Christians seek God as micromanager.

And this is what makes me wish Jesus had said,

> "God does NOT have a plan for your life."

There was no need for Jesus to speak this way in his time. The typical Jewish peasant who listened to Jesus's teachings was not spending his days deciding whether to pursue a career in sheep-husbandry or carpentry. Women were not trying to decide whom to marry and couples were not choosing when or if they should have kids. Certainly, there were decisions to be made, but the excessive individualism of our time was not dominant in their culture.

If you are reading this book, you are a twenty-first-century, privileged person with resources and options absolutely unheard of in Jesus's day and still unheard of in many places on this planet. We hear the phrase "the will of God" and it gets stirred into the minutia of our lives. We lose the Kingdom of God—God's Big Vision—and make the "will of God" a personal matter.

"God does not have a plan for your life."

If we choose first to pay attention to the Big Picture (at least the Big Picture on planet earth), we start to notice that we all have an infinite number of choices and combinations of choices, big decisions and little decisions filling our days. Some of these choices are clearly better—more loving—than others. Some of these decisions are personal, some collective. Mix this with the infinite number of choices and combinations of choices of other people. Their decisions mix with and become factors in our choices. Any moment in our lives is full of such complex choices.

But sometimes a choice is simply a choice.

Jesus didn't teach a formula or set of rules for figuring out what God wants.

Jesus didn't teach that there is a system we enter or an automatic pilot that turns on when we decide to follow him.

A heart open to God—to love—certainly does help us realize the best possible choices in many instances. Paying attention to how our many decisions might affect the Big Picture God offers is certainly a call on our lives. That Big Picture is what Jesus taught—and lived.

Our task is to keep that vision before us and trust that God is present in it all, offering love, wisdom, forgiveness, comfort—freely—into the infinite number of choices and circumstances that shape our lives.

I am reminded of one of the parables Jesus told. Keep in mind that Jesus did not teach in parables with an intention to confuse people. He wanted people to think. More like music or poetry, parables cry out for interpretation, with many possible understandings. Jesus was inviting people to catch a glimpse of something difficult to describe, or try on an idea that had many layers. I offer what is often called "the parable of the sower" as it is recorded in the earliest gospel, according to Mark.

> "Listen! A sower went out to sow. And as he sowed, some seed fell on the path, and the birds came and ate it up. Other seed fell on rocky ground, where it did not have much soil, and it sprang up quickly, since it had no depth of soil. And when the sun rose, it was scorched; and since it had no root, it withered away. Other seed fell among thorns, and the thorns grew up and choked it, and it yielded no grain. Other seed fell into good soil and brought forth grain, growing up and increasing and yielding thirty and sixty and a hundredfold... Let anyone with ears to hear listen!" (Mark 4:3-9 NRSV)

A little later in Mark, Jesus speaks to his disciples in private and explains this parable (Mark 4:13-20). The seeds are God's word and how it is received and/or lost on those who hear. The harvest, then, is the spreading of this word. While many scholars believe this parable to be an authentic teaching of Jesus, many do not believe this interpretation comes from Jesus. Rather, it may come from the early Church and how they understood their work in the world—trying to share the vision of the kingdom.

I find this to be one of many valid understandings of the parable and it is most useful in offering a sense of the early Church and its view of Jesus's teaching. It is also legitimate to hear this parable as if ALL the seeds are churches—some that grow and thrive, some that struggle or survive for a time, some that never quite get off the ground. And it is legitimate to hear the parable as if the field is ONE church and the seeds are all the ways in which people do or do not participate, grow, invite others and so forth.

In all of these understandings, we can start to see variety, choice, circumstance, and we can see the randomness that is offered in this parable through the act of **scattering** seeds. It brings us to another interpretation of the parable in which each of us is a field and the seeds form our existence. In this way, perhaps we can see that God does not have a plan for our lives. God wants each of us to be a healthy field of grain in all ways possible. There is no blueprint for a "perfect" field—simply the knowledge and vision of a full, thriving, beautiful, REAL field. Not every seed is individually placed exactly six inches from the next in some exact form. The farmer SCATTERS the seeds. Wheat fields, like our lives, have some randomness, some spontaneity, some thorny patches, some unexpected twists and turns, some satisfying and unsatisfying outcomes.

Looking at the parable this way, we can see that God is not concerned with our idea of some PERFECT field—our "right or wrong" thinking about every choice and every outcome.

34

Thorns and rocks, pathways and scorching sun are just part of the whole picture when it comes to growing wheat.

If we can let go of the idea that God has a detailed, exacting plan for our lives, then we can let go of the world in which everything is somehow contrived by God, either to keep us in God's will or maneuver us into it if we have strayed.

We can also move away from the worldview that seems popular these days in which there are no accidents. This is the other challenge we face with a micromanaging God. In order to make sense out of difficult and trying circumstances (or amazingly fortunate ones, for that matter), we find ourselves explaining the hard stuff and the good stuff as part of God's plan for us. If God "takes" a child for a reason we can't yet know, it might seem to ease some of the pain of a tragically short life.

If a person wins the lottery or gets that amazing promotion, to thank God for this "blessing" feels somehow natural and humble. But once you start down this road, you either have to claim God is "causing" these kinds of things in everyone's lives or you have to make peace with God playing fast and loose with a few chosen people. I am making a distinction here between an attitude of gratitude for life's delights and a claim that God is specifically creating these circumstances.

I hear all kinds of variations on this:

People are "taken" from us so we can learn lessons of love and courage as a result of their deaths.

People with challenging birth defects are actually "angels" among us.

God has blessed some with good fortune so they will be blessings to others.

Accidents and hard things happen to us to challenge our faith and teach us more about trusting God. Tragedies can be punishments for our sins.

In the same way that some choices are simply choices:

Accidents just happen.
Tragedies just happen—
and so do good things.

There is an arrogance in thinking that everything that happens to you or around you is about YOU personally! To look for meaning in everything that happens to us is really pretty self-absorbed and egotistical.

We DO learn things in this life—at least I hope so.
We grow and change.
We can be transformed by accidents, illnesses, wonderful, unexpected opportunities.

But no one is born into this life just so someone else can learn some lesson.

Life isn't school.
Life isn't practice for something better in heaven.
Life is life!

We CAN learn from anything that happens. In fact, we NEED to learn from our experiences. But the primary point of this learning is to simply discover more of how to love and be loved in the midst of it all.

In my worldview, love is God's nature. Living is about expressing God's nature.

We are how God finds expression. Together, we are God's beautiful wheat fields.

Think again for a moment of those wheat fields as our individual lives in the Kingdom of God, here and now—not perfect, not without conflict or difficulties. Some things go wrong or fall away or never get started. But there is a lot that is wonderful, fruitful, joyful—flourishing in our fields.

Uh-oh. Fire flares in YOUR field!
    A wildfire?
        Has someone tossed a cigarette?
            Was a child playing with matches?
                A natural disaster? An accident?
                Someone's choice?

        Certainly not God's plan.

But when this happens, God's vision calls us to—

Trust resurrection and new beginnings in the midst of anything and everything.

So we heal. We share. We start over. We discover new ways to work together. We choose to offer and receive love—to experience and express God.

This may sound idealistic but the Big Picture IS the ideal. God's vision for us is how God might express and experience love through us—not a plan, but an amazingly compelling picture of what is possible through the choices that shape our lives.

Questions to consider:

1) What are some of the implications of the idea that God would specifically cause bad things and good things in our lives? Describe this God.

2) What is God's role in the difficult places in your life? What is God's role in the easier, more joyful places in your life?

3) If God's overarching vision for creation is the expression of love and beauty—God's very nature—how would you describe humanity's role in this? How do individual followers of Jesus discern and develop their particular roles?

4) If an open heart can help us realize the best possible choices, what can this look like? Do you have experiences you can name where you feel your choices have been led by God?

In your own words: How would you describe God's vision for the world? Everyone walks the path of their choices. Step by tiny step we create ourselves. I think God has provided a chance to learn about ourselves & experience our humanity/humanness. Being miserable or happy is a choice. Being sad is a choice. Being poor is a choice. Learning how to choose is the _trick_.

experiencing love, joy + creation is the goal.

38

Chapter 5 Things I Wish Jesus Said:

"Don't Expect a Miracle."

If we accept the idea that God does not preplan and micromanage our lives (as discussed in Chapter 4), we end up with a lot more responsibility for ourselves and for each other. Where, then, is God in all of this? Why do we pray, sometimes with great hope or expectation? Does God ever DO anything or intervene in any way?

This is where we twenty-first-century followers of Jesus start talking about miracles. God breaks through in extraordinary ways in our lives and prayer seems to be the tool by which those miracles are wrought.

"Expect a miracle" is the confidently placed bumper sticker of many Christians.

For me, the idea of miracles raises many important questions. Just look at accounts of miracles attributed to Jesus throughout the gospels: he heals groups of lepers, a hemorrhaging woman, blind people, deaf people, lame people… He turns water into wine… He raises more than one person from death… He casts out demons…

How did Jesus choose who got a miracle; or did he?

Are miracles of healing different somehow from other kinds of miracles?

Did he ever fail at a miracle or turn someone down?

Why didn't he ever restore an amputated leg?
(a favorite question of atheists)

Did he perform miracles to draw a crowd or make a point, or was the miracle a point of its own?

I don't know if anyone ever raised these questions with him, but I wish he had said,
"Don't expect a miracle."

Centuries after Jesus walked the earth, many Christians have the idea that whenever an especially good thing happens in their lives, it is a miracle—a special gift from God. This is the way they see God moving in the world. Miracles are a gift to the faithful—the prayerful—whether they are praying for themselves or for some non-believing friend or relative.

A miracle can be getting well after being gravely ill or receiving money that you desperately need or finding the way after being lost (literally or metaphorically). A miracle can be walking away from a plane crash or being saved from a burning building.

> It's hard to define a miracle—it's somewhat a
> matter of interpretation, but God intervenes in
> an extraordinary way.
>   We know one when we see one!

This simple understanding of miracles raises many concerns for me.

I have seen many good-hearted people pray faithfully for a miracle of healing, hoping to beat cancer or some other serious illness. In spite of this effort, many of these hopeful people die anyway. Or they have a remission of several months, which they call a miracle, only to succumb again later and die from their illness. Not every faithful person offering sincere prayer gets a miracle—or maybe they get a temporary miracle?

> Giving God "credit" in this way makes God
> seem very fickle.

I have talked with people who have walked away from accidents or disasters in which others have lost their lives. Many struggle with *survivor guilt*, wondering why they lived when others perished. Amongst those who make peace with this are some who conclude they were spared by God in order to have a second chance or to do some special work in the world.

41

Apparently, only SOME people are given special opportunities or intentional second chances.

And are we to assume that it is a lack of faithful prayer that leaves some children homeless or starving? Is it God's decision that some fragile lives don't make it to adulthood and others do? Why does one faithful soul get a much-needed financial reprieve and another not? When we see people without faith receive miracles, does this happen in order to bring them to faith? Or maybe there were simply plenty of faithful people praying for them?

Prayers—anyone's prayers—are woven into all of this understanding of miracles. So, the response to failed prayers for a miracle—an outcome we didn't want—is often, "It simply wasn't God's will."

> I am troubled with this vague understanding of miracles.
> At best, miracles seem quite complicated.
> At their worst, miracles are theologically disturbing.

Once again, it leaves us with a God who chooses to bring ease or special purpose to some and not others. Still, we continue to long for them, pray for them, expect them.

I wish Jesus had said, "Don't expect a miracle."

Let's try to clarify and explain what constitutes a miracle.

I would say this:

Miracles are positive encounters with the mystery of God, making the impossible seem possible in the moment. They are extraordinary and sacred moments of grace that bring joy and transformation.

Furthermore, they seem remarkably random and, *most often*, they cannot be easily explained. I say this because some things that have been considered miraculous in the past can now be explained by science or medicine; or we can look back at a chain of events and see how something seemingly inexplicable unfolded for the good. No doubt some things we find miraculous now could someday be similarly explained in the future.

The fact that we can or can't find explanations simply doesn't matter.

It remains a miracle if a positive encounter with the mystery of God brings healing or transformation into any lives or circumstances.

With these ideas in mind, I believe in miracles.

But I also believe that understanding miracles has much to do with how we understand prayer. This is where things seem to get a little theologically fuzzy. While at times there seems to be a direct link between someone experiencing a miracle and the intensity of prayer that surrounds the person, that may be more misleading than helpful in comprehending miracles.

I often say to my congregation:

The content of our prayers doesn't really matter.

We can speak or be silent.
Our prayers can be full of askings or gratitude
or complaints or laughter.
They can be selfish or selfless, peace-seeking or
even vengeful.

It doesn't matter.

It is the open, honest heart that connects us to God—to the source of all love. It is the outpouring of the truth that opens our hearts, making space for God's love to enter into and flow out of our lives. At the end of his days, I was praying that I would have more precious time with my father. I am sure he was praying that his life end quickly, sweetly and coherently. The content of neither prayer mattered, nor changed the course of his illness. We were being totally honest and open with God. And in that honesty, love guided our times together and we both felt a deep peace. But I believe it is possible that the love flowing through our prayers may have moved into places and people who had little or nothing to do with our situation.

We tend to think in very linear terms: I am praying for you and you are the beneficiary of that prayer. We don't always consider that love—God's actual presence—when freed in the world through our open hearts, can flood the world with miracles and moments of transformation anytime, anywhere!

Jesus was so open to God—that flow of God's love in his life—that people saw God in him and through him and they opened their hearts as well. That in itself must have been a pretty intense, positive encounter with mystery!

Jesus wasn't just a miracle worker—he was a miracle.

We look at him and we can see how amazing and surprising a miracle is—and at the same time, he made it seem so simple.

Jesus—no one I know of lived a life more fully in the love of God. So his miracles seem to be, and in a way are, quite extraordinary.

But he asked us to follow him, learning to live passionately and freely, following his teachings. He told us we could do what he did and more. When we simply pray, pouring out the truth of who we are and how we feel, our hearts open and love flows in us and through us and the outcomes are beyond our control. Miracles happen—even when we don't see the results.

Our own lives may offer an encounter with the mystery of God to others! If we can bring joy or transformation into someone's life, then we no longer need to hope for miracles or expect miracles. We, like Jesus, ARE miracles...

Questions to consider:

1) Have you been party to a miracle? How would YOU define "miracle" based on your experience?
2) Would you agree or disagree that the content of your prayers doesn't really matter? Why?
3) What is the danger or harm in expecting miracles?
   Are there times in which we, as followers of Jesus, should expect miracles?

4) Finding twenty dollars in the street may be a miracle for one person but this may barely catch the eye of someone else. How do our personal circumstances impact our perceptions of miracles?

In your own words: As in Question 1 above, how do you define "miracle"?

Chapter 6 Things I Wish Jesus Said:

"Never forget that you are playing God."

Building on the idea explored in the previous chapter that each of us, like Jesus, can BE miracles in this life, the question arises: what does this look like? What is our part in making that possible? I think the answers to these questions begin to take shape when we recognize that we are all playing God—all the time.

Many of us can recall vividly the Terri Schiavo medical case that drew so much public attention in 2005.

> After years of family fighting over whether or not to remove a feeding tube from Terri, who was diagnosed to be in a persistent vegetative state—

after years of fighting in the courts at the local, state
and, eventually, federal levels—
    after an astonishing amount of debate in the press,
    even internationally,
Terri Schiavo's feeding tube was removed and five days later
she died quietly in a Florida hospice. The autopsy showed
that much of the interior of Terri's brain had been dissolving
into liquid and that there was absolutely no hope she would
ever have recovered in any way from a mindless, waking-
sleep state.

The fight to keep Terri alive—in the family, the courts and the
press—had many layers and tactics, but mostly it came down
to this:

> We have no right to remove the one tool that
> could keep Terri, and all hope for her future,
> alive. To remove the tube and let her die is to
> *play God and interfere with the will of God.*

The religious right was strongly represented in backing this
position. So were far more liberal figures like Jesse Jackson. I
remember thinking at the time how strange it was that people
of faith would find <u>death</u> to be the worst thing that could happen to Terri Schiavo.

Did they expect a miracle? Did they fear for her soul? Did
they fear for their own souls if they didn't fight for her life? I
wondered.

But I wondered also—

Wasn't it also "playing God" or interfering with God's will to put the feeding tube into Terri in the first place?!

Whether it's antibiotics or surgery, radiation or physical therapy, or herbal remedies, aren't we playing God just about any time we make medical discoveries or offer treatments that change the course of what would occur if a person was left untreated?

Medicine is just one arena in which our intelligence and curiosity can shift the course of human events. We tamper with the "natural" course of things constantly: eyeglasses, laser surgery, corneal implants, the engineering of food through grafting and breeding techniques, the construction of whole cities below sea level behind levies, the capacity to fly, to move through outer space and explore the far reaches of the cosmos, the Internet and the virtual reality it offers. The list is endless.

I think if Jesus were among us today, he would say,

"Never forget that you are playing God."

Some Christians think of "playing God" as taking power in their own hands in ways that may interfere with what God has designed or orchestrated—thus changing the outcome of God's will—God's plan. I do not see it this way.

We have already explored, in an earlier chapter, the convoluted thinking that makes God the micromanager of our day-to-day, moment-to-moment experiences in this world. There are no puppet strings attached to us and no singular specific outcomes planned for our lives. Rather, God is a presence—a loving presence, in and through all that occurs. God holds a vision for what is possible, even in the darkest of circumstances, and offers a way of living in the world (which one way I would describe the Kingdom of God).

Decisions along the way are ours to make, individually and collectively. We are empowered with the pleasure and responsibility of choice.

We are also empowered with amazing creativity.

This creativity can be directed toward curing cancer or designing fuel-efficient cars or knitting baby clothes or writing poetry or solving math problems or exploring the depths of the ocean.

This same creativity can be used to design bombs or rob banks or lure a child into a stranger's car. It can be used to cheat on taxes, manipulate a spouse or plan a military assault.

In all these ways, we are playing God, making choices that change the course of events in ways great and small. We should never forget that. We have been given great freedom and responsibility.

"Playing God" is not the same as "being God."

We aren't God.

Playing God is more like improvisational theater or jazz.

We all have roles to create or instruments to play around an important theme. When we use our imaginations and our bodies, our talents and our hearts, we create like God creates, but in human form—in the world. When we consciously choose to expand and explore around God's theme of unconditional love, then goodness and beauty, peace and justice are created. When we reject the theme, our creativity pulls us in other directions. The play unravels. The music is lost.

This is why it is important for us to never forget that we are playing God.

This isn't a perfect metaphor—all metaphors have their limits. The apostle Paul offers the "Body of Christ" as a way of describing this same thing. Each of us is a distinct and important part of Christ's body, and this body is God's loving presence in human form—first in Jesus, now in us. Like the improv group or the jazz combo, the Body of Christ means we are none of us going it alone.

I think when we play God in the way I am describing here, we make creative choices with loving hearts. Sometimes the choices are not clear. Life is not a black-and-white experience. It is not about making "perfect" choices. It is about making loving ones.

Keeping this in mind, playing God is never about taking our creativity, or the worldly powers that come our way, or even the time we have, and using these things for selfish purposes—on a big or small scale. It is important to stay focused on the vision of God's love; then playing God is about the power of that love for one another—on any scale. Mother Teresa said it well:

> "In this life we cannot do great things—only small things with great love."

Jesus showed us the power of this great love. He showed us how to play God in this world. He did it so well that when we see Jesus, we see God. He trusted God's presence and always made his choices with an open heart. He changed the world and he invited others to do the same—to build the Kingdom of God.

I find this to be an important theological insight, one I cannot say often enough:

Jesus was so open to God—to love—that when we encounter him, we experience what God (love) looks like in human form. He invited his followers to be open in the same way—to live and love as he lived and loved!

Two thousand years later, the invitation stands.

Never forget that in this life, we are all playing God. Choose to be the power of love in human form.

Questions to consider:

1) Can you share any examples from your life experience in which you felt the reality that you were playing God in some way?

2) The phrase "playing God" may be problematic for you. Beyond doing improvisational theater, making jazz, and being the Body of Christ, can you think of other ways to describe this amazing power and creativity we have at our disposal and how it relates to its source in God?

3) We do not always have the foresight to recognize the full impact of our actions. Can you name some times and circumstances in which human intentions and creativity have gone awry?

4) Talk more about differences between "playing God" and "being God."

In your own words: If you believe God moves in your life, describe what this means.

Chapter 7 Things I Wish Jesus Said:

"You won't find heaven with a compass."

There is a description of heaven and hell that I heard when I was young that has stayed with me over the years.

> In hell, everyone is seated at long tables with a great feast set before them. Every person has a long fork tied to one arm and a long spoon to the other—so long that you cannot bend your arms in such a way that the utensils can reach your mouth. Hell is full of continuous hunger and frustration; you cannot be satisfied or enjoy any of the feast set before you. Everyone sits there crying out, screaming in hunger, pain and continuous frustration.

In heaven, the setting is essentially the same, with everyone at a feast, long spoons and forks attached to their arms, making it impossible for them to feed themselves. But there is much laughing and smiling and celebration in heaven—as everyone feeds someone sitting across from them or nearby.

These little scenarios stick with me because they describe heaven and hell mostly as attitudes or states of being. Heaven is that state of love, compassion and care for one another, while hell is a state of self-absorption where one doesn't even see the possibility of kindness toward another.

But somehow, for us to grasp concepts like these, we seem to need a sense of place—a physical context. Heaven is entered by rising up to pearly gates in the clouds, where there are streets of gold. Hell is a fiery pit into which one is thrown—a dark, bottomless abyss full of fire and smoke. We want God, or the absence of God, located in our three-dimensional world, locking God in time and space with us.

This is understandable historically, but as twenty-first-century people with an expanded base of knowledge about the shape of our three-dimensional world, we KNOW that heaven is not, as ancient people thought, a few miles above the earth. We KNOW that the earth is a sphere and that the cosmos it moves in is vast indeed. In fact, traveling at the speed of light, Jesus could not yet have "ascended" to the known edges of the universe. Albert Einstein tells us that our universe is expanding into "previously nonexistent space." Wow! Apparently, God is still creating. Simply by knowing that the earth is round, we realize there is no "below-the-earth place" for a fiery hell to be located. And I don't think even the most literal believers think hell is located in the tiny, molten center of our planet. While these "up" and "down" understandings of heaven and hell may have made sense in a much earlier time, they make no literal sense today. Yet, even knowing this, many Christians cling to the notion that heaven and hell are physical locations.

> I wish Jesus had said, "You won't find heaven
> with a compass."

Forget about geography when you try to comprehend heaven. If we don't locate God in some distant place but allow God's presence to be anywhere, then love, God's essential nature, can live and move in us right where we are—in this life. What I would call the *soul* is that loving presence in us, whether we are aware of it, open to it or allowing it to flow from us. This *soul* is like a little spark from a greater fire. In the absence of our three-dimensional bodies, there is absolutely nothing that separates this spark from the greater fire—from love—from God. This, in my understanding, is heaven—complete union with God, encumbered by absolutely nothing—existing outside of time and space.

Forget about geography when you think about hell. Hell is when that soul, that little spark, is separated from its source—from love—from God.

> And that can be possible anytime—
> most certainly here and now.

We can say "no" to God in this life and cut ourselves
off from love.
We are free to refuse God at any time for a moment, a
season, a lifetime.

People can also experience hell not of their own choosing. A
person can be cut off from love by being isolated, tortured
or smothered by hate, where persons or powers in this world
force people into hellish solitude. Being cut off completely
from love is hell—no matter how one gets there or how long it
is experienced or where one is located. We can be denied love
at any time for a moment, a season, a lifetime.

What happens, then, if you are someone who chooses to say
"no" to God's presence your whole life? Or what happens if
you never had a chance to say "yes" to love in this lifetime?
Does this mean you then stay in hell forever? Would a loving God refuse love to one who is essentially part of God's
very self? No, I don't see hell as a part of God's ultimate
intention, which I believe is to express love in and through
us, bringing forth a kingdom or world where love reigns.
If love is truly greater than any other power, then love will
overwhelm even the most lost, skeptical, awful persons we
can name. If love is greater than any other power, then it
can heal and rekindle any smothered little flame that never
stood a chance in this life. Ultimately, love receives it all.
Heaven is the name for that, too. And you won't find it with
a compass.

You may have a different understanding of heaven and hell.
The point here is to recognize how our understandings of God

can be freed by allowing God to be God beyond our limited knowledge of time and space.

This letting go of geography—setting aside the compass—to speak of God's presence also applies to the Kingdom of God, which some people think is just another name for a heavenly afterlife abode.

Jesus's early followers thought that God, in some very concrete way, would bring heaven (from three miles above) down to earth and locate God's self in the heart of things, smiting all enemies, bringing peace and justice and ruling from an earthly throne. There would be a new Jerusalem and Jesus (God incarnate) would judge and rule from that throne in this sort of new capital city.

> This is ironic. In teaching about the Kingdom of God, Jesus did try to be clear that it wasn't a PLACE.

> He used parables—about a mustard seed or a precious pearl or a hidden treasure or leaven in bread or a beaten man lying in the road to talk about the kingdom.

> He told stories with the intention of opening listeners' minds and hearts to a new understanding—a new way of being, in any circumstances—in all circumstances.

> In the synoptic gospels (Matthew, Mark and Luke), he tells questioners that they won't see signs because "the Kingdom of God is already among you." (An equally good translation in English is "within you.")

He seems to be pointing to the Kingdom of God as RELATIONSHIPS—

—relationships with him, with God, with each other, with those we have called enemies, with neighbors…

Jesus is offering a new paradigm. Instead of ushering in an apocalypse and a new capital city, Jesus was teaching the Kingdom of God as a far more subtle and subversive force in the world, already present in and among people, no matter where they are or what their circumstances. He was teaching and demonstrating the power of love not in the future, not in some particular place, but in the moment. And the irony is that early followers of Jesus, with that long history of looking for God to come from the clouds to violently fix things, shift Jesus right back into that earlier paradigm—where he is the judge and bringer of wrath for the wicked. And the Kingdom of God is the place for the faithful. Sigh. If only Jesus had said, "You won't find it with a compass."

Thinking of the Kingdom of God as a limited location diminishes it. If anything can transcend all the geographical boundaries and barriers we have erected in this physical world, it is the vision of God's kingdom.

I can hear Jesus say—

"God is not concerned with the location and size of your church buildings."

"God is not concerned with whether you live on the 'right' side or the 'wrong' side of the tracks."

"God is not concerned with who has the historical rights to the holy lands."

"God is not concerned with where you draw and re-draw the borders between your nations."

"All the lines you draw in the sand, dividing up territories and relationships—these lines dangerously distort God's vision, God's kingdom."

If we let the artificial lines we have drawn and all the ways we measure and evaluate our physical world define how we believe God moves, we have turned Jesus's message of the kingdom upside down, holding him in that old paradigm.

Sometimes we forget that the Kingdom of God is about loving our neighbors, and we let our geography get in the way of seeing who our neighbors really are.

And sometimes our geography interferes with following Jesus—to work for peace and justice and to offer love and compassion wherever it is needed.

And sometimes our geographical stuff gets in the way of letting God be GOD...
...who loves us without conditions or boundaries...

...who has shown us what that love looks like in the life and teachings of Jesus Christ.

...who is still expanding the universe into non-existent space.

So, I can hear Jesus say, "You won't find heaven with a compass—or hell, or God's kingdom!"

God is not limited by our maps of the world.

Questions to consider:

1) If you let go of heaven and hell as actual places, how does this impact your view of "eternal life"?
2) Is the fact that the universe continues to expand into non-existent space possible evidence that God is still creating? If so, or if not, what other evidence might there be of God's ongoing creativity? Does God know any boundaries or limits?
3) What do you think of the idea that the Kingdom of God is based on relationships?
4) There is a need in this life for healthy borders and boundaries. Can you name some of these? How do we reconcile these needs with the notion that God transcends all borders and boundaries?

In your own words: Talk about heaven.

CHAPTER 8 THINGS I WISH JESUS SAID:

"VIOLENCE WILL NEVER BRING PEACE."

Dietrich Bonhoeffer was a notable German theologian whose work, along with that of many other Christian scholars of his time, is still an influence and building block in how many Christians understand God. But he is perhaps most remembered for his activities and, ultimately, his death during World War II in Nazi Germany.

He was a man of peace in the deepest sense, understanding that the teachings of Jesus about the Kingdom of God referenced a world in which God's peace and justice reigned, not as a result of human warring, but, in fact, quite the opposite.

He believed Jesus exemplified and taught how his followers should ENGAGE the world—not retreat from it or make war on it.

This Kingdom of God—the reign of God—would not come through violence.

Rather, it would come through the power of God to change human hearts.

Bonhoeffer was an early and outspoken critic of Hitler. Sometimes he was a lone voice amongst the leadership in German churches. He did all he could to create a church movement to actively oppose Hitler, and he often put himself at risk often in his efforts to halt the Nazi movement. He continued this resistance from 1933 until his death by hanging in a Nazi prison camp in 1945.

Ironically, this man of peace was hanged as a conspirator
in an assassination attempt on Hitler.

And, indeed, Bonhoeffer was guilty.

He did not deny that he was party to more than one attempt to kill Hitler. He admittedly supported and kept secret plans that, had they succeeded, would have resulted in Hitler's death.

He went to his own death acknowledging his guilt and his need for God's forgiveness in the matter. Bonhoeffer had taken stock of the sorry, sorry state of the world and determined that things had gone too far—that there was no longer any non-violent way to stop Adolph Hitler; to kill him would be the lesser evil.

He went to his death admitting human failure in this struggle.

He went to his death trusting God's grace for himself in the matter.

I offer this story because it points so clearly to the tremendous challenge of following Jesus in a world that can be so rapidly overwhelmed by fear and what can only be called "evil." For Bonhoeffer, to do nothing seemed the greater sin. He believed Christians must ACT in the world to stop injustice, making the best decisions they can, trusting God in the midst of pathways that are not clear—not black and white.

Doing the best that he could, however, Dietrich Bonhoeffer fully realized that Hitler's death, or any other violent solution, for that matter, would never bring a final peace, a lasting peace—the peace of God. A violent solution falls short every time.

This is important.

And this is why I wish Jesus had said,

"Violence will NEVER bring peace."

Violence may offer a temporary solution.
It may create a moment-in-time effective defense.
It may totally change the course of human events.
History shows all these things to be true.
But violence will never bring true peace.

What do we mean by "peace"? Dr. Martin Luther King described peace as:

"…not the absence of conflict but the presence of justice" (justice being that effort to level the playing field so all persons have opportunity for food, shelter, freedom, real joy).

I believe he was spot-on in being sure we don't view peace as an absence of conflict. Conflict, differences, disagreements, edgy places—these are intrinsic to a world full of choices. It is how we navigate those conflicts that matters. When I consider the life of Jesus, I would define peace in this way:

Peace is the presence of love in the midst of conflict.

Or, one could also say:

Peace is the absence of violence in the midst of conflict.

What do I mean by "violence"?

I would offer this working definition—

Violence is any aggressive behavior that causes harm in order to impose one's will on another.
It stems from a misuse or abuse of available power.

This means that violence could be deeds or words.
It could be interpersonal or international.

It could be aimed at countries, peoples, individuals
—even toward the planet itself!

Understood this way, violence can be seen as a
primary description of sin.

Theologian Walter Wink addresses this topic at length. In his
book *Engaging the Powers,* he writes of "the myth of redemptive
violence," the idea that somehow we can fight or even fiercely
argue our way to a lasting peace of any kind.

The same history that demonstrates the frequent but temporary
shifts towards peace brought about by force also shows us that
there is ALWAYS fallout (sometimes quite literally) from violent
solutions.

There has never been an enduring peace when violence has been
used, even to halt injustice or oppression or crime. Violence will
always leave wounds on all sides: physically, emotionally, spiri-
tually—these wounds live on from generation to generation.

And violence will rise again in some form—overt or
subtle.

Perhaps Wink's understanding can give us insight into our
violent world:

The death penalty has not stopped violent crime. And crime-
victim families often report that a perpetrator's death does not
really bring peace of mind or satisfaction. Sometimes, it leads
to new trauma and confusion.

Gangs fighting gangs, claiming neighborhoods, "protecting turf"—this offers a glaring example of how violence horrifically perpetuates itself.

Through violence, governments may be stabilized or overthrown;
borders may be maintained or totally reconfigured;
conflict may cease at some level;
revenge may be exacted;

> but a true and lasting peace is never achieved in this way.

Our Civil War reunited the United States by force. Visit the South and you will quickly sense that there are many unhealed wounds after all these many years.

Using atomic weapons in Hiroshima and Nagasaki brought the surrender of Japan, but now, in addition to all the individuals directly affected by these bombings, we all remain fearful of who may next develop and use these instruments of death.

Violence has settled nothing in the complex struggles between Israel and Palestine (to name just one such ongoing nightmare).

We went to war more than a decade ago after terrorists flew airplanes into the Twin Towers and the Pentagon, yet it would be difficult for us to name what has actually been achieved by all the warring in the time since then.

The wounds of wars, all kinds of wars—personal, global, physical, verbal, spiritual, emotional—are passed along in various ways.

We did eventually stop the Nazi movement in World War II, but the psychic wounds of soldiers coming home from that war (or any war) have left scars and open wounds on so many lives. Once it was called "shell shock." Now we call it post-traumatic stress disorder. I call it the failure to bring peace.

But let me return to Dietrich Bonhoeffer for a moment. His story demonstrates that there are times when violence seems to be the only choice we have. Once Hitler got such a strong foothold in Europe, Bonhoeffer could not discern any viable choices to stop him that were not intrinsically violent. But he didn't fool himself that this was going to bring a lasting peace, and he saw human failing as a huge factor in Hitler's rise to power. He felt the need for grace and forgiveness. He also saw no other way.

This is important.

Violence should be the absolute last resort—because there will be fallout, and it will never bring real and enduring peace.

Can we imagine a world in which warring is the very last resort?

> Ah, you may be thinking that the bad guys will
> surely win.
> If we don't fight, then we must hide or run.

Fight or flight…
This is the pattern humanity has fallen into: in primitive civilizations, in Jesus's time, pretty much all the time. Fight or flight. Winners or losers.

If we don't fight—
If we don't run or hide—
What DO we do?

Jesus did teach and live another way—the way of true peace—but it seems to have gotten lost.

Let's look back for a moment.

When we read the apocalyptic images in our Bible, we see how, before Jesus's time, the hope was that God was going to fight a last BIG battle and put a violent end to all oppression and injustice.

Unfortunately, early Christians slid Jesus into that fighting role and they began to wait for him to return as King, the one who would demolish the bad guys in a final judgment.

That's what people thought, hoped and prayed for.
Many still do.

To me, this shows the limits of human experience and imagination.
We can't seem to think of another way—or our instinct to merely survive wins out over any new thinking. If the only way we can imagine to bring peace is zapping the enemies, then that becomes Jesus's job.

The saddest thing about this image of Jesus as the final warrior/judge/king is that it is contrary to the core of his teachings.

Jesus elaborates on his most difficult commandment—to love your enemies—in the Gospel According to Matthew (5:38-48). If you read this passage, it becomes clear that Jesus is not talking about how one FEELS about one's enemy. He is commanding his followers to BEHAVE in new and unexpected ways.

And at the heart of these teaching comes those very familiar directives to turn the other cheek, and give the coat and the cloak off your back and walk the extra mile. A quick read of these teachings coming to us through our twenty-first-century lenses might suggest that these are timid or passive interactions.

But in Jesus's time, his words no doubt brought shock and even laughter. Consider the Roman laws and ancient culture:

If someone backhands you with his right hand and you turn the other cheek so he could then hit you with the left, you have created an embarrassment for that person. The left hand was considered unclean (used for personal hygiene) and was never used in public.

If a Roman guard took your coat, that pretty much left you with just your underpants. If you took that off and offered it as well, you would be naked and that was completely unacceptable.

Roman law allowed a soldier to force you to carry his bag for a mile—only a mile. If you insisted upon going a second mile, you would be causing him to break the law.

In all three cases, the actions point to the injustice of the situation and subvert the oppression inherent in the context.

In all three cases, the actions claim the high moral ground.

In all three cases, the actions are bold and unexpected—and seemingly foolish.

In all three cases, the actions are nonviolent.

Finally, in all three cases, the person who behaves in these ways is truly at risk. Nonviolence is dangerous.

If you track Jesus's words and behavior all the way through to his arrest, trial and execution, he opposes injustice, he claims the high moral ground, he is bold, his actions are unexpected and seemingly foolish…

　　　…and it costs him his life.

He did not defend himself.
　　　He did not defend God.
　　　　He was, quite literally, defenseless,
　　　　　trusting God alone.

This means that in whatever way you may personally understand the resurrection, it is fair to say that the power of God—

the love of God—was stronger than violence, stronger than death itself.

So, Jesus's life, death and resurrection give us a glimpse of the Kingdom of God—a kingdom full of bold and foolish people who will not fight for what is just, but will courageously risk themselves in the faith-filled hope of healing the world and bringing true peace.

True peace—something violence can never achieve.

Questions to consider:

1) Can you think of any "sin" that is not, in some sense, violent (as violence is described in this chapter)?
2) When in your life have you felt "peace" by your own definition? How do these experiences compare to "peace" as it is defined here?
3) What, if any, might be life circumstances in which violence may rightly be the first choice?
4) By behaving nonviolently, as Jesus did, you may actually provoke violence. Discuss this irony.

In your own words: Describe Jesus's work in the world; what he saw as most important.

Chapter 9 Things I Wish Jesus Said:

"Love is never about gender."

EVERYONE seems to have something to say about homo-sexuality—everyone except Jesus.

The gospel record shows he talked a lot about economic jus-tice and money. He spent a good deal of time on the topic of the Kingdom of God and what it is like to be part of that. He made commandments about loving—neighbors, self, enemies.

But he didn't talk about romantic love;
     and he didn't talk about homosexuality—
          at all.

As part of the Church in the twenty-first century, I can think of no topics that are causing more pain and upheaval within our walls. And, from my view, that struggle has spilled out the church doors and helped fuel the oppression and condemnation of gay, lesbian, bisexual and transgender (GLBT) people in American culture and beyond.

Whatever biases and confusions exist about sexuality and gender, we in the Church have made matters worse. We've done this by letting the Bible be used SELECTIVELY and IRRESPONSIBLY. It is indeed the weapon of choice in a war on GLBT persons—a weapon that gets used by serious and deeply committed Christians, as well as people with no meaningful connection to the Christian faith. The Bible gets used to condemn GLBT persons—out of ignorance, irresponsibility and sometimes absolute malice.

I have to count myself among the countless Christians who spent many years simply accepting the loudest interpretations of scripture AS SCRIPTURE. It is what I was taught early on in my church. Looking back, as I entered young adulthood, I found myself unconsciously trying to figure out how to follow Jesus and, at the same time, ignore these BIG BIBLICAL TRUTHS. Too many people I knew were slowly but surely coming out of closets everywhere!

I heard a lot of "love the sinner, hate the sin" talk. I certainly loved the sinners but I had a hard time seeing, yet alone hating, the sin. This began to create a serious split within me—a split between what I KNEW to be true about good people I loved, and what the Bible apparently and authoritatively said about them. It was enough to make me doubt all I thought I knew about God and walking with Jesus.

Fortunately for me, I got "saved"—more than once.

I got saved by some courageous pastors who did their best to speak out in a church culture that really wasn't yet equipped to listen to a more in-depth reading of scripture. I watched these pastors navigate seas that were pretty much uncharted in church. Not all of them kept their pulpits. Their courage touched me, even though the Church seemed to hold fast to its earlier, harsh teachings.

I got saved by watching my aging parents hang in there as their church community began to split over this topic. My parents were of a generation that did not talk publically about "private matters" of any sort and they were WAY out of their comfort zone. But they stayed with their church even as many of their friends left. Their courage touched me.

I got saved again in seminary when I was offered the opportunity and the skills to read the Bible critically, closely and holistically. I felt convicted of my ignorance. I felt grace. I found some courage of my own.

Mostly, I've been saved by GLBT people in my life, who still love and live openly as followers of Jesus—forgiving those who trespass against them, claiming their places in the body of Christ, even when the body isn't so sure they are welcome. I have learned so much about grace and about trusting God. I have learned something about how to stand up in that grace and trust.

More recently, I have been saved yet again—by science. There is such a growing body of evidence that calls into question all the solid lines we have drawn to define ourselves by gender or by sexual orientation. I suspect that even the terms "straight," "gay," "lesbian," "bisexual" and "transgender" have built-in obsolescence and limited usefulness as we learn more.

Our gender-identification is composed of so many factors BEYOND our outer anatomy: internal organs, brain chemistry, body chemistry, hormones, genetic makeup and more. We are a conglomeration of these ingredients. This is true in ALL of us but is more obvious in its complexity among persons who identify themselves as transgender or transsexual. It is a rare person who could be identified as purely male or female.

This is important.

> Once this science-based understanding is accepted and we begin to see gender-identification as a kind of continuum, all the lines we draw about sexual expression and attraction begin to fall away as well.

In all these ways, I've been saved. I am grateful.

I have not walked away from church or from Jesus or from the God of love.
I have reconciled what LIFE demonstrates and teaches with what the Bible can
      offer on this and many other subjects.
I have been freed to stand up with and, if needed, on behalf of my GLBT friends
      and colleagues in and outside the church.

Still, it would have been much easier if Jesus had simply said,

"Love is never about gender."

Now, of course he didn't say this. When we think about love and gender, a whole host of things pop up for us. We must be talking about romantic love. In Jesus's time, couples may have fallen in love and had many moments we might define as "romantic" (check out "Song of Solomon" in the Hebrew Bible), but "coupling" seems to have been more about procreation and practicality.

This is important.

Marriages were hugely socioeconomically motivated and were qualitatively different from what we call "marriage" in our time and culture. It's a little tough to think "romance" when a woman is essentially property. It's tough to talk about romantic love when she must marry her brother-in-law if her husband dies. Contrary to the popularity of the phrase highlighted in many conservative churches, "God designed marriage for one man and one woman," men could indeed own more than one wife.

With these things in mind, the whole glamorization of biblical marriage that attempts to match the serial man/woman monogamy of our time is really not accurate.

I'm not trying to solve the current public debates about who gets to get married, who gets to have a legal union, who gets left out altogether and why this matters so much in so many different ways to all kinds of people.

I'm not trying to make a case justifying any and all sexual behavior, crossing any and all gender/sexual identifications. There is no justification ever for sexual behavior that is hurtful or nonconsensual or abusive of power.

I want to talk about RELATIONSHIPS—relationships in which people really care about each other, ongoing relationships that include a responsible and loving sexual component.

And I wish Jesus had talked about it.

We don't have evidence of Jesus ever being involved in any relationship that included a responsible and loving sexual component.

We never hear of him being torn between his personal life and his work. He did go off and pray alone about temptations in his life, but nothing states these temptations were about an urge to become sexually active outside the bonds of marriage (which was indeed a cultural taboo). We know that both men and women followed him—traveled with him and loved him dearly. We don't know if anyone among them was a "groupie" with a crush.

Nothing in scripture about Jesus and his followers gives hard evidence that anyone was IN love with anyone else, at least not in a way that was named or acted upon. There's just no "romance" around Jesus...

...and not much talk about loving, sexual relationships in his teachings.

He does seem to care about marital fidelity, while stating clearly that you pretty much can't help but lust occasionally, anyway (Matthew 5:27-28).

We know that at least one of Jesus's followers was a married man, Peter, although we only meet his mother-in-law (Mark 1:29-31, Matthew 8:14-15, Luke 4:38-39).

He cautions men about divorcing their wives (Mark 10:11-12, Matthew 5:31-32, Luke 16:18). One has to take into account that a divorced woman was left pretty much without recourse or resources, and Jesus seems to be taking this on as a justice issue for women, rather than making an attempt to encourage more loving marriages.

But, seriously, a summary of the life of Jesus using all four gospels offers very little about loving, sexual relationships of any kind. And, with a few exceptions (like "Song of Solomon"), the whole of scripture is pretty light on the subject of loving, sexual intimacy.

Still, a little parade of highlighted scriptures marches off the pages of the Bible with trumpets and drums, shouting about the "sin of homosexuality."

It is not my intention in this chapter to expound on the handful of texts that are used to condemn GLBT relationships and identities. The favorites include: Genesis

19:4-8, Leviticus 18:22 and 20:13, Deuteronomy 23:17, 1Corinthians 6:9-10 and 1 Timothy 1:9-10. You can find volumes written on these and other verses—on the Internet, in bookstores—volumes.

Instead, I want to make a few general comments that might shed light on attempts to read these passages. We again visit the challenge of understanding and applying biblical texts in our time.

TRANSLATION MATTERS:

Some more recent translations of the Bible—*The New International Version*, *The New Living Translation* and *The New King James Version* come to mind—use the word "homosexuality" in translating to English.

Funny thing—the word "homosexual" was coined in the nineteenth century! The term emerged from the newly forming psychological community as it worked to explore and document human behavior.

There is no such word as "homosexuality" in Greek or Aramaic or Hebrew.
    No such word.

Rape. Prostitution. Orgies. Ritual sex. Abusive sex.
One of these words or phrases would be more specific and more accurate in every case.

CULTURAL CONTEXT MATTERS:

The Jewish community was always concerned with strengthening their numbers—building up their strength—to gain and maintain their freedom.
Men shouldn't "waste their seed." PROCREATE!

Thus the emphasis on *men and women* being married and fertile. I have no doubt love could enter the mix, but the point was making babies.

In that ancient context, there was no place for upholding loving, sexual relationships between people of the same gender.

In twenty-first-century life, population growth is actually a problem; in our country, much sexual activity EVEN AMONG MARRIED PEOPLE is not about procreating. Population ex perts are glad about this!

We need to acknowledge our hugely different cultural context.

YOUR CONSCIOUS CHOICE MATTERS:

Many of us grew up amongst good church people who ingrained in us not only careful attitudes about the Bible but REALLY careful attitudes about sexual expression of ANY kind. This makes stepping away from biblical literalism feel like a particularly dangerous leap even if we are not generally biblical literalists.

Very conservative Christians in our time don't practice slavery or isolate a woman during menstruation, even though you can find scripture that supports these practices.

Christians today eat shellfish and faithful women cut their hair, even though you can find scripture that prohibits these practices.

We make reasoned choices about these matters. But when it comes to talking about sexual relationships, gender and the Bible, it seems some unconscious switch gets flipped.

This means a *conscious choice* is sorely needed to bring clarity.

As a follower of Jesus, I feel compelled to consider his teachings on love.

Yes, we are to love one another.
Yes, we are to love our neighbors.
Yes, we must learn to love our enemies.

Sure, there are different kinds of love—many would associate the word *eros* with love between partners.

"Eros" is that "I'm in love" kind of love. Eros is a magnet of feelings, including sexual attraction.

While this certainly plays a role in bringing two people together, I continue to keep my focus on what I offer couples when they want to get married—about the way in which feelings aren't enough.

LOVE is action—intentional action that offers another person patience and grace and humility and honesty (oh, just go to 1 Corinthians 13—it is a good list!).

This love is self-sacrificing and unconditional. I tell them they have to keep choosing it, day after day, again and again because it is what sustains and grows relationships.

It can be called "agape"—love like God's love for us. (I distinguish this from "phileo," which would be used to reference shared interests, friendships—what is sometimes called "brotherly love.")

Agape love is genderless and boundless, intended to heal and nurture
        and never cause harm.
I am not aware of anyone who can thrive without experiencing it.
All kinds of people share agape love in this world with all kinds of people.
As followers of Jesus, we embrace and affirm the spread of this selfless love.
        It is what Jesus lived and taught. It is
    what God offers everyone.

"Eros," "falling in love," is not bound by our gender stereotypes.
All kinds of people "fall in love" with all kinds of people.
This can be confusing.
This may make some people uncomfortable.
It happens all the time.

But, for an "eros" relationship to endure between two people, they must share that "agape" love as well.

The result can be a joyous and enduring union (although surprisingly rare in this life).

This union of "eros and agape" for male-and-female couples is unanimously accepted by all followers of Jesus. It often ends up in marriage.

It is quite another matter for persons who presently carry the labels "gay," "lesbian," "bisexual" or "transgender." While there are pockets of tolerance within the "Church universal" and within Western culture, there is often limited acceptance and no real justice for couples who don't match up to the classic male/female model.

If you choose to attach moral, biblical sin to their love-based relationships, you are joining the ranks of many who say there ARE limits to God's love and how it can be manifested in this world—that there are limits to the ways genuine caring and love can be expressed.

It is a position you can choose. It has been chosen by many Christians.

There is another perspective. It requires a conscious choice to affirm that love truly holds no bounds—that all persons were made to express love and that gender and sexual identities do not create limits on how that love may be shared.

It is only this choice that will bring in our GLBT brothers and sisters who are standing just outside the doors of many churches—being told, however gently, that they just don't have it quite right.

True, Jesus didn't say, "Love is never about gender," but if he were here today, I suspect he would be standing outside the churches with all the GBLT folk, waiting for us to figure out what "love" really means.

Questions to consider:

1) What childhood/youth messages did you receive that may impact your views on GLBT issues and concerns?
2) Is the understanding that gender and sexual identifications rest on a continuum new to you? Is this helpful? Explain.
3) What are the fears that make matters of gender and sexuality so difficult to talk candidly about in church? What do you think helps further such conversations?
4) In what ways do you see the struggles of GLBT persons as justice issues?

In your own words: Describe your perspective or position on loving homosexual relationships.

AFTERWORD

When I finished my sermon series on "Things I Wish Jesus Said," I asked people to let me know if there was anything THEY wish Jesus had said.

I got lots of answers.

Many people wish Jesus could answer some of the questions they have—like these:

> Was your mom REALLY a virgin?
>
> When DOES life actually begin?
>
> Is there life on other planets? Have you visited those places and brought them God's message of love? Or arc we it?!
>
> Are there ghosts? Is there reincarnation?

Others have statements they wish Jesus had made—like these:

"Nobody's perfect—including me."

"Men, get in touch with your feminine side—show a little vulnerability."

"Every person is a child of God. There are no 'chosen ones.'"

"God does not look like us."

"Eternity is NOT about time."

"Science is not God's enemy."

It has been nearly two thousand years since Jesus walked the earth. The world is a very complicated, often overwhelming place. It is natural for us to wish for more wisdom and direction from him.

Still, this is merely wishful thinking. He can't say more.

We cannot hear his voice today, or catch his body language and inflection.
There will be no press conferences or rallies.
We cannot post his new comments on Facebook or video clips on YouTube.

…merely wishful thinking.

But, honestly, there is nothing wrong with wishful thinking
because it IS thinking—

> thinking about Jesus and the things that really matter
> to us as his followers.

Wishful thinking is, after all, the work of head and heart together, a kind of dreaming—imagining…

And these dreams and imaginings certainly can shape and
clarify our faithful attempts to discern what Jesus might say
or do.

They guide us as we try to be a loving presence in this crazy
world.

They keep before us the BIG PICTURE of what is possible.

Somehow, in our wishful thinking, our dreams and imaginings, Jesus's voice comes through in our lives.

INFLUENTIAL SOURCE MATERIALS

I am sure you noticed there are no footnotes or endnotes throughout this book. It isn't possible to make many specific references because my theology has been shaped over time by all kinds of reading, conversations and experiences.

I recommend and have used for this book the *New Revised Standard Version of the Bible (NRSV).* There are many translations available these days, but the *NRSV* continues to be widely respected and accurate.

I offer the following general references that have been especially influential:

Borg, Marcus, *The Heart of Christianity: Rediscovering a Life of Faith,* HarperCollins, 2003

The Five Gospels: What Did Jesus Really Say? The Search for the Authentic Word of Jesus, Robert Funk and the Jesus Seminar, HarperCollins, 1997

Mesle, C. Robert, *Process Theology: A Basic Introduction,* Chalice Press, 1993

Sahajananda, John Martin, *You Are Light: Rediscovering the Eastern Jesus,* John Hunt Publishing, 2003

Spong, John Shelby, *The Sins of Scripture: Exposing the Bible's Texts of Hate to Reveal the God of Love*, HarperCollins, 2005

Weatherhead, Leslie D., *The Christian Agnostic,* Abingdon Classics, 1990

Whitehead, Alfred North, *Process and Reality,* Free Press, NY, 1985

Wink, Walter, *Engaging the Powers: Jesus and Non-Violence; Discernment and Resistance in a World of Domination,* Fortress Press, 1992

Ideas for Additional Reading

General interest:

The Battle for God, by Karen Armstrong
Christ for the 21ˢᵗ Century, by Ewert Cousins
Dancing on the Edge, by Richard Holloway
Doubts and Loves, by Richard Holloway
God: A Guide for the Perplexed, by Keith Ward
Honest to God, by John Robinson
The Heart of Christianity: Rediscovering a Life of Faith,
        by Marcus Borg
Process Theology: A Basic Introduction, by C. Robert Mesle
Re-thinking Christianity, by Keith Ward
You Are Light: Rediscovering the Eastern Jesus,
        by John Martin Sahajananda
Your God Is Too Small, by J.B. Philips

Chapter 1 "Don't believe everything you read."

Kerygma and Myth, by Rudolf Bultman
Myth and Christianity: An Inquiry into the Possibility of Religion
        Without Myth, by Rudolf Bultman and Karl Jaspers
Rescuing the Bible from Fundamentalism, by John Shelby Spong
The Sins of Scripture, by John Shelby Spong

Chapter 2 "It's not about me."

The Birth of Christianity, by John Dominic Crossan
Honest to Jesus, by Robert Funk
Jesus as Precursor, by Robert Funk
Meeting Jesus Again for the First Time, by Marcus Borg

Chapter 3 "I didn't come to save you."

A Search for What Is Real, by Brian McLaren
The Inescapable Love of God, by Thomas Talbot
Lost Christianity, by Jacob Needleman
The Religious Case Against Belief, by James P. Carse
The Secret Message of Jesus, by Brian McLaren

Chapter 4 "God does not have a plan for your life."

The Cloud of Unknowing,
        14th century English author unknown
I and Thou, by Martin Buber
Man's Search for Meaning, by Viktor Frankl

Chapter 5 "Don't expect a miracle."

To Love and to Pray, by Roberta Bondi
Practicing the Presence, by Brother Lawrence

Chapter 6 "Never forget that you are playing God."

No particular suggestions here, although of interest might be an essay by JRR Tolkien entitled "On Faery Stories."

Chapter 7 "You won't find heaven with a compass."

See previous books of general interest.

Chapter 8 "Violence will never bring peace."

The Girard Reader, essays by Rene Girard
The Joy of Being Wrong, by James Alison
Letters from Prison, by Dietrich Bonhoeffer
Prison Poems, by Dietrich Bonhoeffer
A Testament of Hope, by Martin Luther King, Jr.
Trilogy by Walter Wink:
    Engaging the Powers:
        Discernment and Resistance in a World of Domination
    Naming the Powers:
        The Language of Power in the New Testament
    Unmasking the Powers

Chapter 9 "Love is never about gender."

Homosexuality and Christian Faith:
Questions of Conscience for the Church, by Walter Wink
Is the Homosexual My Neighbor?
Revised and Updated: A Positive Christian Response,
    by Letha Dawson Scanzoni and Virginia Ramey Mollenkott
The Sins of Scripture, by John Shelby Spong
Undergoing God: Dispatches from the Scene of a Break-in,
    by James Alison

CPSIA information can be obtained at www.ICGtesting.com
Printed in the USA
LVOW01s1737031013

355313LV00018B/1322/P